Everybody at King Saul's palace knew about David the shepherd boy. He had killed the giant Goliath. And he played beautiful music on his harp.

After the battle with Goliath David went
to live at King Saul's palace. There he
met Jonathan, the king's son. They liked
one another at once. They were best
friends and shared all their secrets.

David was famous. All the Israelites liked him. He was so brave.

The king became very jealous.

'They will be making him king next!' he thought to himself. 'I must get rid of him. Even Jonathan loves him best.'

One day David was playing some music for the king, to cheer him up. Suddenly King Saul picked up a spear and threw it at David.

David jumped out of the way. The spear stuck quivering in the wall. David ran away from the palace.

Jonathan was very sad when David went away.

'Everybody loves David,' Jonathan told King Saul. 'We can all see that he is growing up to be a great man.'

But that just made the king hate David more. Jonathan told David that Saul was trying to kill him.

David knew that God would take care of him. He had promised that one day David would be king of Israel.

But still Saul tried to get rid of David.

9

One night there was a great feast in the palace.

'How can I come to the feast if the king wants to kill me?' David said to Jonathan. 'If he asks where I am, tell him I have gone to see my family.'

Jonathan promised to tell the king.

At the great feast that night King Saul
asked where David was. When Jonathan
told him, he went into a rage.

'Why are you taking sides with
David?' he said. 'You are my son. You
should be king when I die. If I don't kill
David, he will become king.'

Jonathan went to tell David.

'You must never come back while my father is alive. He will kill you.'

David did not know where to run but he knew God would show him.

He went to live up in the hills where
there were some caves. Some of his
friends went with him.

David knew that he was in danger,
but he was sure that God would look
after him.

The king kept trying to find David, to kill him. One day King Saul sat down to rest, just outside the cave where David was hiding. David crept out and cut a piece off the king's robe.

As the king walked away, David called
out to him, 'Why are you trying to kill
me? I came very close to you just now,
but I did not hurt you.'

The king saw that David was holding
a piece of his robe and he knew that
David was right.

But before long the king forgot that
David had not hurt him on the hillside.
He went hunting for David again.

This time David crept into the king's
camp at night. He took the spear that
was stuck in the ground at King Saul's
head.

In the morning he called out, 'King
Saul, where is your spear?'

It was gone. Saul knew that once
again David could have killed him. So
Saul went away.

One day David heard news of a terrible
battle. King Saul and Jonathan had been
killed by the Philistines.

It was the saddest day of David's life.
He missed his best friend very much.

The Israelites crowned David king. God's promise had come true. There were still many battles to fight. But they knew that God would help David to be a good leader.

David captured the city of Jerusalem. There was great celebration when he brought the special box which held God's laws into the city. David himself danced for joy.

David wanted to build a temple for God in Jerusalem. He made all the plans. But there were still many battles to fight.

David and his army fought all the enemies of the Israelites and at last there was peace.

King David ruled over a great nation.
He loved God all his life. He did not always obey God. But when he had done wrong he was sorry and always asked God to forgive him.

God kept all the promises he had made
to King David.

'Your son, Solomon, will be king after
you,' God said. 'He is the one who will
build that temple for me.'

The Lion Story Bible is made up of 52 individual stories for young readers, building up an understanding of the Bible as one story — God's story — a story for all time and all people.

The Old Testament section (numbers 1–30) tells the story of a great nation — God's chosen people, the Israelites — and God's love and care for them through good times and bad. The stories are about people who knew and trusted God. From this nation came one special person, Jesus Christ, sent by God to save all people everywhere.

The story of *King David* occupies a big slice of the Old Testament history books, 1 and 2 Samuel. David also wrote or collected many of the Psalms. And his reign is covered again in 1 Chronicles. Unlike Saul, David proved to be 'a man after God's own heart', even though he did many things that were wrong.

Although God did not let David build him a temple in Jerusalem, as he longed to do, he made him a special promise. The line of kings that David began would not die out. And one day God would send a very special king, a descendant of King David, to save his people. The name of that king was Jesus.

The next story in this series, number 20: *Solomon's golden temple*, is about King David's famous son.